Cybersafety

Surfing Safely Online

Joan Vos MacDonald

Enslow Publishers, Inc.

40 Industrial Road   PO Box 38
Box 398   Aldershot
Berkeley Heights, NJ 07922   Hants GU12 6BP
USA   UK
http://www.enslow.com

For Sylvan, Amanda, and Emmeliah

Library of Congress Cataloging-in-Publication Data

MacDonald, Joan Vos.
    Cybersafety: surfing safely online/Joan Vos MacDonald.
        p. cm.
    Includes bibliographical references and index.
    ISBN 0-7660-1580-7 (hard)
        1. Internet and teenagers—Juvenile literature. 2. Computer crimes—Prevention.
    3. Internet—Safety measures. I. Title.
HQ799.2.I56 M33   2001
025.04′0835—dc21   00-011621
                                                        CIP

Printed in the United States of America

10 9 8 7 6 5 4 3 2 1

To Our Readers:
We have done our best to make sure all Internet addresses in this book were active and
appropriate when we went to press. However, the author and publisher have no control
over and assume no liability for the material available on those Internet sites or on
other Web sites they may link to. Any comments or suggestions can be sent by e-mail
to comments@enslow.com or to the address on the back cover.

Trademarks: Most computer and software brand names have trademarks or
registered trademarks. The individual trademarks have not been listed here.

Illustration Credits: © Corel Corporation, pp. 6, 34, 42, 51; Enslow Publishers,
Inc., p. 17; Library of Congress, p. 41; SafeKids Web site, p. 11; Skjold Photos,
p. 48.

Cover Photo: © Skjold Photos; Background © Corel Corporation.

Contents

1 Cybersafety 5

2 How the Web Ensnares 15

3 The Golden Rules
of Good Computing 29

4 Cybercrime 37

5 How Teens Can Get Parents
to Respect Their Privacy 45

Chapter Notes 53

Glossary 57

Further Reading 59

Internet Addresses 60

Index 63

1

Cybersafety

Not many people want to log on to the computer with someone looking over their shoulders, checking to see which sites they visit and who they are talking to. Yet there are online dangers to be aware of and take precautions against. The Internet is where half the nation's teens already spend hours each day and the number of teens online is expected to rise to almost 80 percent by the year 2004.[1] By learning more about cybersafety and demonstrating Internet know-how to their parents, teens can prove that they do not need much cybersitting. When teens learn the rules of the road, they may be able to cruise the information superhighway and avoid online dangers.

Dangerous Detours

A recent interview in *YM* told the story of Heather Moore, twelve, who loved to surf the Net, mostly visiting chat

When teens learn the basics of cybersafety, they can cruise down the Internet information superhighway without fear.

rooms. In a chat room, Heather met Charlie, who said he was sixteen and a high school sophomore. Heather was sure she had met her soul mate. She gave Charlie her phone number and address. Charlie started to send her gifts, such as jewelry, stuffed animals, posters, and books.

Charlie suggested exchanging snapshots. Then Charlie asked for more graphic photos, such as shots of Heather in her underwear. Heather's mom found Charlie's letter requesting the photographs and wrote to him to say he should never contact Heather again.

Shortly after that, Heather's mom got a call from a detective who was investigating Charlie Hatch for stalking boys and girls on the Internet. The detective told the family that Charlie was actually a thirty-six-year-old man named

Charles Hatch. Charlie was arrested and then sent to federal prison for six and a half years. But when he was out on bail, Heather was frightened. Charlie knew where they lived and where she went to school.

When visiting the Internet, be very careful never to give out any personal information. Because she trusted someone she met online, Heather placed herself and her family in a dangerous position.[2] Meeting someone in a chat room can provide a false sense of having a lot in common. It can also create a situation in which people exchange personal information with strangers they would know not to trust in real life.

Rather than being too trusting online, some teens take advantage of other people's trust. These teens make the mistake of thinking that what happens online is a game, that no real people can be hurt by online actions, and that they will never get caught. That is what can happen when teens use the Internet to make quick money, threaten people, or vandalize Web sites.

For four New Jersey high school students, hacking (getting into and bypassing security codes that protect) a credit card system seemed like a challenge right out of the movies. The teens obtained credit card numbers by tricking America Online and Earthlink subscribers into downloading files via the Internet. According to the *Associated Press*, the downloaded files enabled the teens, ages fourteen to sixteen, to get the passwords, addresses, phone numbers, and credit card numbers of people in several states.

With this credit card information, the cyberscammers charged $8,000 worth of merchandise to other people's accounts. They had their purchases sent as "gifts" to houses where they knew no one was home. It seemed like a computer game at which they would never get caught. However, these New Jersey high school students were caught and now face criminal charges that include fraud, conspiracy, and credit card theft.[3]

A Road Map

The Internet has been compared to a big city. The safest way to explore this electronic city is with a road map showing the location of potential trouble spots and safe detours. Safely navigating cyberspace means knowing which areas to avoid and what types of decisions might lead to trouble.

For example, a smart driver knows that it can be dangerous to pick up a hitchhiker. A teen with a basic knowledge of navigating the Internet knows that telling a stranger she meets on the Internet her name and address is just as dangerous as it might be to give it to a stranger on the street. By learning such cybersafety tips, teens can use the Internet to meet people from around the world and to tap into a world of interesting and entertaining information.

Teens navigate the Net to find information for homework, get tutorial help, play chess, learn about favorite celebrities, and meet pen pals who share interests. Net know-how can help a teen plan a trip (calculate the route, the amount of gas needed or the cheapest air fare, find out where to stay, and what there is to see), explore the family tree, or download a fascinating game.

"A couple of years ago, having a friend with access to the Net was a rare occurrence. Now, finding somebody who doesn't is quite a feat," said David Thelan, a sophomore in Saginaw, Michigan, in a column that appeared in *Computer World*. Thelan uses the Net to play games, listen to music, look up song lyrics, and e-mail his favorite bands at their Web sites.[4]

Many teens feel confident about their Net navigational skills. Since they are probably more computer literate than their parents, they may be insulted at the notion that their parents want to supervise their Web activities. However, parents are influenced by news stories about teens who were molested or harassed by people they met online, were arrested for e-mail threats, or learned how to build bombs at a Web site.

While 38 percent of the parents answering a May 1999 *Newsweek* magazine survey said they sat with their eleven to fifteen year olds while they went online, only 9 percent did so when their children were ages sixteen to eighteen.[5] Sixty-eight percent of the teens answering a recent survey by *Time*/CNN said their parents knew little or nothing about the Web sites they visited.[6] Also, teens have more physical freedom and more financial resources than younger computer users to act on the information they get on the Net.

Information Superhighway Caution Signs

Talking in a chat room can place a teen in a vulnerable position. Web-surfing worries can range from fear of physical danger to scams to computer viruses that destroy a computer's hard drive.

While the Internet is ideal for meeting others with similar and unusual interests, it is also an ideal medium for taking advantage of teens, since it can be difficult to tell if people really are who they say they are online.

Teens can place themselves in physical danger by arranging to meet someone who seems friendly and sympathetic online but may actually turn out to be a pedophile (adults who prey on children sexually). According to the

Here are several examples of the types of dangers teens may face:

- A teen may give away information about where she lives and put herself in physical danger of being stalked, physically attacked, or abducted
- A teen may lose her privacy and be bombarded by unwanted e-mail messages
- A teen may be harassed
- A teen may get the idea that it is okay to harass someone else through threatening or demeaning e-mail messages
- A teen may get into legal or financial trouble by hacking or sending an e-mail
- A teen might harm his or her computer or computer programs by downloading a computer virus in an e-mail message

National Center for Missing and Exploited Children, the Internet is a favorite hangout for pedophiles.

Even in teens-only chat rooms, fellow chatmates may just pretend to be other teens. Someone claiming to be a fourteen-year-old girl may be a forty-year-old man. By giving out personal information, teens can make it easy to be found by someone who wants to hurt them. The National Center for Missing and Exploited Children reports 10,601 cases of sexual victimization of children, including child pornography and cases in which a pedophile tried to arrange a meeting with an underage victim.[7]

Spam

Giving up privacy online can also expose a person to a practice known as spamming, in which e-mail message banks get so overwhelmed with messages from advertisers that the person has to sort through piles of junk e-mail just to get to legitimate e-mail. These messages can range from get-rich-quick schemes—which sound too good to be true because they are—to subtle scams, such as a Web site for children and teens that collected personal information promising it would be anonymous, then sold that information to marketers.[8]

"I do get whole piles of spam mail. Somehow my address got added to those nasty spam lists. It has trailed off, but I used to get, on the average, two e-mails a day from spam

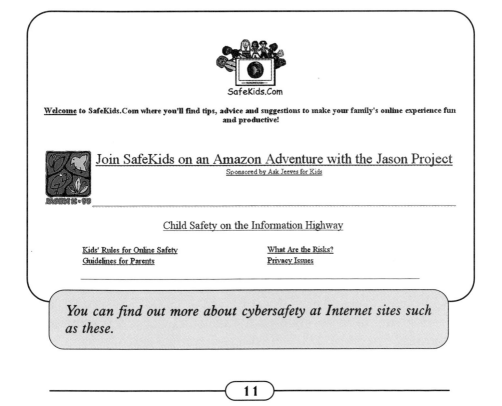

SafeKids.Com

Welcome to SafeKids.Com where you'll find tips, advice and suggestions to make your family's online experience fun and productive!

Join SafeKids on an Amazon Adventure with the Jason Project
Sponsored by Ask Jeeves for Kids

Child Safety on the Information Highway

Kids' Rules for Online Safety
Guidelines for Parents

What Are the Risks?
Privacy Issues

You can find out more about cybersafety at Internet sites such as these.

lists. It is really annoying, because I might accidentally delete something I should read," said Austin Lang, a sixteen-year-old high school junior.[9]

Messages are posted in news groups, Internet discussion groups for people who share a special interest (also called bulletin boards or news forums), or chat rooms (electronic places to meet and talk with people from around the block or around the world, in real time). Through these messages, teens may also be exposed to material that makes them feel uncomfortable, such as messages that are sexual, violent, or hateful.

"If you go into chat rooms for like a second and then open your mailbox you get like thirty porn mail things. It's really annoying. I just delete them, but some send more later on. One day I was just so fed up, so I e-mailed the people back. After that, I kinda stopped getting it, though sometimes I still do. One time it was really false advertising. It said 'Win a free Furby' and so I opened it to see what it was and it was porn mail," said Emi, a fourteen year old from Cortlandt, New York, who likes to visit chat rooms. When asked if she is eighteen, old enough to sign on, she has said yes. No one checks to see if teens are telling the truth.[10]

Although teens may be asked if they are eighteen when they sign on to many chat rooms, no actual proof of age is required. By pretending to be older, teens may subject themselves to adults-only advertising. Advertisers clearly do target underage teens because an advertisement claiming you can win a free Furby is aimed at a much younger age group than eighteen year olds.

Flaming

Teens can also get flamed, that is, receive threatening messages or messages that make them feel uncomfortable, through personal e-mail or in chat groups. Sometimes this happens because people forget their cybermanners, but it is often done intentionally and may even be a crime. For example, it is a federal crime to send teens messages or images that are obscene, lewd, filthy, or indecent with the intent to harass, abuse, annoy, or threaten.[11]

Cybercrimes

In November 1999, the U.S. House of Representatives, a branch of Congress, passed a bill extending the law against stalking (harassing or injuring someone) into cyberspace. According to the National Center for Victims of Crime, one out of five harassment victims is now cyberstalked with threatening e-mail.[12]

Since e-mail threats were sent by the teenage school-children who then shot twelve students, one teacher, and themselves in Littleton, Colorado, in 1999, such threats are being taken much more seriously.[13]

It is also possible for teens to hurt other people and get themselves in legal or financial trouble without realizing that they are doing so. By sending an e-mail message that could be interpreted as harassment or imply a threat, a teen could earn a visit from the police.

That is what happened to a teenager known by the online name of Chameleon, who boasted that by hacking into the Department of Defense Web site he had been able to copy some software vital to the nation's defense system. According to an article on hackers in *Vanity Fair*, this boast attracted the attention of international terrorists, who paid him a thousand dollars for the software.

This criminal transaction was eventually reported to the Federal Bureau of Investigation (FBI). As an indirect result of Chameleon's e-mail boast, a dozen FBI agents stormed into the nineteen-year-old hacker's bedroom one morning while he slept and woke him by pointing a pistol at his head. Although Chameleon was ultimately not arrested, he is not likely to hack and boast about it again.[14]

Although hacking into the electronic system of a school or business might seem like a challenging game, it is considered breaking and entering or vandalism and laws are being passed to make it easier to prosecute.[15]

Other dangers also lurk on the Internet. Computer users of any age may encounter the annoying and potentially expensive problem of accidentally opening up a computer virus that can damage or destroy a computer. A hazard of Internet research can be getting untrue or biased information from an Internet source. Not all Internet sources provide true or accurate information.

2

How the Web Ensnares

According to one Internet saying, "On the Net nobody knows if you are a dog." Or a wolf in sheep's clothing. The faceless nature of Net communications can make it easier to take advantage of those who are more vulnerable. On the Internet, many things are often not what they seem. A computer user must be careful not to become a victim.

Wolves in Cool Clothing

Not being able to tell who anyone really is on the Net makes it easier for pedophiles to meet and take advantage of teens. Pedophilia is one of the most widely publicized and persistent dangers on the Net.

"Twenty years ago your molester would have been in the park," said Detective Steven McEwan, a high-technology investigator with the San Jose Police Force in an interview in the *San Francisco Chronicle*. "Today, they come into your home via the computer."[1]

Chat rooms, usually organized around a topic, such as music or a hobby, can be good places for pedophiles to meet teens and—sight unseen—win their trust. One effective way to establish this trust is for a pedophile to pretend he is another teen. To be convincing, pedophiles sometimes read teen magazines, watch popular television shows and movies, and learn about popular music. Since people cannot see each other when they talk on the Net, it can be hard for a teen to tell if his or her new best friend is a wolf in disguise.

After winning a teen's trust, predators may begin to introduce sexual topics and use child pornography to make a teen think that others take part in such activities. They may ask teens to perform certain sexual acts and ask them to videotape or photograph themselves in the act. Predator and victim may exchange phone calls.

After a while, the predator may try to arrange a face-to-face meeting. When the teen discovers that the person is not another teen, he or she may feel so embarrassed about what has already happened and how easily he or she was fooled, that he or she may feel the need to get even more involved, says Parry Aftab, an international corporate and cyberspace lawyer, in *A Parent's Guide to the Internet*.[2]

It is important to remember that it is always the adult in these cases who is at fault and who has broken the law. Federal laws make it clear that enticing anyone under eighteen to take part in any kind of sexual activity or child pornography is a serious crime. That request should be an immediate warning sign and should prompt a teen to report the incident to a trusted adult, law enforcement officials, or a confidential hot line.

According to the National Center for Missing and Exploited Children (NMEC), teens can do a lot to protect themselves from predators. First, online teens should always keep their identity private and choose a screen name that does not reveal anything. Using the name AnnS15, for example, may lead someone to conclude your name is Ann and you are a fifteen-year-old girl.[3]

Because e-mail addresses are listed in online address directories, an address can be used to track down where a

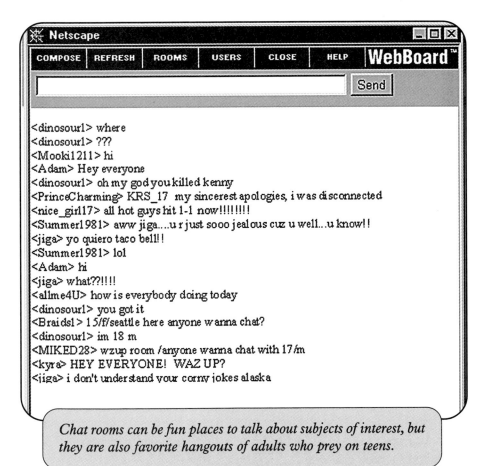

Chat rooms can be fun places to talk about subjects of interest, but they are also favorite hangouts of adults who prey on teens.

person lives. If a person knows how old his or her e-mail pen pal is and where the person lives, it is easy to figure out where the pen pal goes to school. It may also be possible to see what the person looks like by "leafing" through an online directory of that school or a photo album of that person's place of worship. Did that person make the honor roll or score in a recent soccer game? Much information can be gained online.

Online articles from a local newspaper may fill in a few other facts. A knowledgeable user of Internet resources can take a few facts and use them to draw a map to that person's house. People may ask for e-mail addresses for legitimate reasons—such as for marketing purposes—but sometimes those addresses are used to victimize others.

Of the millions of children surfing the Web, the National Center for Missing and Exploited Children has so far only documented one hundred thirty cases of a child who has left home or a predator who has tried to get a child to leave home as a result of an encounter on the Internet.[4] However, the number of cases of pedophiles trying to get children to meet them is growing, says Jim Russell, an assistant district attorney in Denver, in an interview with the *Denver Post*.

"I have [a] stack of cases on my desk, pedophiles who allegedly attempt to lure children from their homes over the Internet," said Russell. "The problem is not going away. It's only getting worse."[5]

To stay safe, teens should never get together with someone they meet online, unless the meeting is supervised. Discuss the possibility of meeting a cyberbuddy with parents. Perhaps a first meeting can be set up that is supervised by parents. If the other person is really a teenager, he or she will not be surprised by parental concern.[6]

Harassment—Get the Message?

People sometimes send offensive, discriminatory, or annoying messages designed to disrupt chat rooms.

"A lot of the time people flood the screen with messages. They'll say the same thing and repeat it over and over, which really only works where the chat room scrolls down but it's still incredibly annoying. That way you miss a lot of posts. Sometimes I ask them to stop 'cause that's not cool. Sometimes they stop and that's cool and sometimes they don't," said Alyson.[7]

The next step is usually to ignore the offender, but that may not always work. If the messages become too annoying or threatening, or if someone sends messages or images that are obscene, lewd, filthy, or indecent, the next step is to contact the site's postmaster (postmaster@whatever.com) or the Internet service provider (ISP). Or you can contact the National Center for Missing and Exploited Children. The person who has sent the harassing message may have his or her account canceled and if they have broken the law he or she may be prosecuted. If you are in a chat room, you can also sign off.[8]

That is also one of the reasons that teens should never give their password to anyone else. That password can be used to get into a chat room and harass another person. That harassment can result in the cancellation of the owner's account, even if he or she is innocent.

Spam and Scams

Just as snail mail may arrive wedged in the mailbox between inches of junk mail, unwanted e-mail, also known as spam, may clog up an e-mail box. Some of it may be advertising, some may be pornography, and some may contain scams that try to get teens to invest time and money—with no return. Here is an example of a spammed scam, which Austin Lang, sixteen, found in his mailbox, but he was wise enough not to pursue.

"You have the opportunity to partake in the most extraordinary and powerful wealth building program! I will show you how you can earn $150,000.00 this year from the comfort of your home. If you're skeptical, that's okay. Just make the call and see for yourself. We will teach you how to amass wealth, protect that wealth, and show you how to make that wealth work for you, rather than you working for it."[9]

When a person subscribes to an e-mail list on a subject that interests him or her, unwanted e-mail usually accompanies requested information. These lists are really discussion groups to which messages and responses are e-mailed instead of being posted on a bulletin board. Such groups may send out more than forty messages a day. When subscribing to any e-mail service, it is important to save the computer-generated message detailing how to unsubscribe if there is too much incoming mail.[10]

Milk and Cookie Time?

Some Web-browsing programs create files called cookies that are left on the computer user's hard drive after he or she has visited certain sites. Cookies help Webmasters (Web managers) track and record information about visits to the Web site. It can make online activity faster because some information about a buyer is already available.

For example, information about previous purchases may make it easier to recommend something new that the buyer might be interested in. The file into which cookies are deposited is contained within the software used to browse the Internet. Several of the most recent versions of browser software can notify a Web surfer before the site places a cookie on the computer. Some browsers will let the user deactivate the cookie file or let the user check and delete information in the cookie file.[11]

Manufacturers also use other methods to get information about online shoppers. Many Web sites require visitors to fill out a questionnaire when they visit the site. That helps them learn more about the people who visit the site, gather information about how to sell more, and provide better service. If a company learns that people of a specific age group visit their site, they may make their site more attractive to that age group. Reputable Web merchants post a privacy policy that explains how they use any data collected from visitors to the site.

Credit Card Transactions

While the Internet offers a wide variety of goods and services, deciding which are legitimate may require some research. Before sending money to anyone on the Internet—to buy something or to contribute to a charity— it is a smart idea to find out where the money is being sent and whether the company or organization is reliable. It is a good idea to stick with Web merchants or companies that exist outside of the Web, except for well-known organizations such as amazon.com or eBay. To check a company, contact the Better Business Bureau or the Direct Marketing Association. Those organizations list complaints against companies.

Credit card information should only be given over secure lines (lines that are encoded to keep other people from being able to read the card number). Some Web browsers will let users know if a site is secure. For example,

Protecting Your Privacy

Feel anonymous online? When computer users log on, the companies on the sites may get access to personal information that users may not want to share. Here are some places privacy could be invaded.

- Signing up at a free membership site. Some sites offer free Internet access in exchange for showing ads to visitors. Some of the banner ads that run across the top of the screen when a Web page is accessed may deposit a "cookie" on the hard drive of visitors' computers.[12]

- Using a credit card online. Credit card numbers have been stolen by hackers. Be sure to use a secure line that is set up to protect your credit card numbers.

- Using a debit card online. A checking account can be cleaned out. Be sure to use a secure line.

- Sending a credit card number or other personal data such as a social security number via e-mail. E-mail is not secure.

- Using a real name and address when posting messages invites spam.

both Internet Explorer and Netscape Navigator display a padlock icon on secure sites.[13]

Because hackers have broken into online stores and stolen credit card numbers, more retail sites are installing filtering security software known as a firewall to keep hackers and computer viruses out. This type of software oversees all communication between a company's internal network of computers (intranet) and outside networks such as the Internet.[14]

Suspicious Web Sites

Buyers are not the only people who need to beware. Information found at many Web sites may be misleading—and in some cases maliciously false. At some sites, information may be presented as if it is true and complete, but certain facts may be left out or slanted to prove a point of view. Even with the best intentions of remaining objective, a Web site will promote the view of the people who sponsor it and will generally only include facts to support that point of view.

Always consider the source of the information, suggests Vince Distefano, author of *Child Safety on the Internet*.[15] For example, a Web site created by the maker of a new drug may discuss the advantages of trying the drug out on animals before it is tried out on people. The creators of this site would see the testing on animals as a good thing because it might rule out any bad reactions people might have.

The description of this testing would include very different facts and a very different point of view than if the site were created by an organization dedicated to the protection of animals. These people might focus on the welfare of animals and see animal testing as a bad thing.

Some sites have deliberately falsified information to promote their point of view. As with any other information source, teens should not automatically believe everything they read.

Domain Names

Another way to decide how trustworthy a source of information is may be to consider the ending known as a domain name. The domain name may identify whether the site creator is a company or a nonprofit organization. Could

---

Here are a few tips to help sort fact from fiction:

- Put things in perspective. Check who is sponsoring the site, where the information—including any statistics—comes from, and consider why whoever created the site may be promoting this information. Does someone, some thing, some cause come out looking better or worse? For example, a Web site promoting a certain political party probably will not say anything good about its rivals.

- Be observant. If the site highlights new developments and mentions only one product, do more research. It may be promotional material distributed by the manufacturer. Lots of different products may do the same thing equally well.

- Be thorough. Research more than one source. How does the site's information differ from others on the same subject? Check at least three sources.[16]

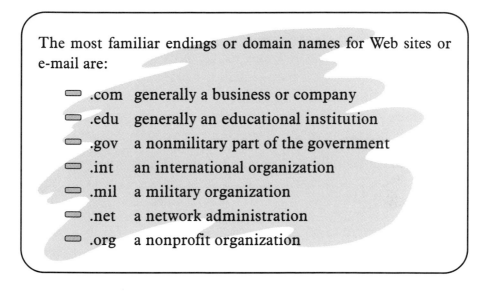

The most familiar endings or domain names for Web sites or e-mail are:

- .com   generally a business or company
- .edu   generally an educational institution
- .gov   a nonmilitary part of the government
- .int   an international organization
- .mil   a military organization
- .net   a network administration
- .org   a nonprofit organization

a company have an ulterior motive for publicizing certain information? Could the site creator have a reason for seeing a situation in a biased way? Information found on the Internet is only as reliable or unbiased as its source.

A site that ends in .com is a company. If it is a cereal company and offers tips on eating a healthy diet, it will probably mention cereal as a healthy food choice. Cereal may be a healthy food choice, but it is not necessarily always that easy to separate fact from advertising bias.

Sites That Promote Hatred

Some Web sites promote hatred and racism. Hate groups use these sites to teach teens to hate those described as being different and sometimes as not quite human. Some teens may find it easier to hate those considered different, rather than confronting problems such as trouble in school, a need for more money, or troubled relationships with parents and friends. When people feel uncomfortable about being able to handle their own problems, it is often easier to find someone else to blame. A 1999 CNN poll identified more than fourteen thousand racist, anti-Semitic, or other hate sites on the Internet—and an increasing number are being aimed at young people.[17]

Such Web sites may feature dangerous propaganda, such as the claims that certain groups of people are inferior and should be hurt, killed, or denied their rights.[18] Often these bigoted site creators cannot find any other way to state their hate-filled ideas.

These groups claim that they have the right to say whatever they want and express their point of view, but an increasing number of search engines are no longer providing access to these groups, so the search engines will not be associated with that point of view.

Screening Systems

Parents or school administrators may install screening software on their computers to discourage children from visiting certain sites. These systems work two ways. They may either block sites that contain disturbing subject matter, such as pornography, or only let users access sites that have passed inspection.

Screening software can be set up on a home computer or requested through some Internet service providers. The software can also be customized to a specific situation. It can be used to block incoming information such as e-mail; to screen specific information being sent out, such as a phone number; or to block online searches altogether. Some screening software lets parents adjust the levels of protection as children mature.[19]

Screened-out subject matter routinely includes violence, nudity, sex, and profanity. Some systems screen for intolerance, homosexuality, gambling, and any sites that glorify drug use, but the definitions of what is acceptable vary from system to system.

Critics say that the greatest fault of these systems is that they often work too well. A site may land on the bad list because it includes a keyword that is controversial. For example, a site dedicated to helping kids quit smoking may be on the same screen-out list as a site that tells kids all about the delights of cigarettes. A site talking about new research aimed at curing breast cancer or a page with recipes using chicken breasts for chicken parmigiana may wind up on the unacceptable list just because the word "breasts" was used.

Even the best programs will not block out all the dangers of cyberspace, so even with these programs in place, it is important to use good judgment and critical thinking.

Finding Help

Since the Internet is like a vast city, someone has to patrol for cybercriminals. That is how the CyberAngels were launched. These cybercops, coordinated by Internet legal expert Parry Aftab, patrol the Internet and report any sites that look like they harbor illegal or unacceptable Internet activity. Besides protecting children from Internet abuse, they pressure service providers to enforce their terms of service. Reporting illegal activity to an agency such as CyberAngels, or to law enforcement agencies, is always much safer than confronting the criminal directly.[20]

Both CyberAngels and the National Center for Missing and Exploited Children have online crime hot lines, so that a crime witness can report a crime confidentially while still online. Certain Internet service providers also have sites set up at which consumers can report complaints. When witnesses and victims of online crime speak up and get help, they make it easier for authorities to find the criminal and prevent that criminal from hurting other people.

An increasing number of police departments are learning about the Internet and several states are starting special divisions to investigate cybercrime. Even if a police department does not have a computer crimes division and cannot, for example, find out who is sending a teen harassing e-mail, that police department will know about knowledgeable national organizations, such as the FBI, which may be better equipped to help.[21]

3

The Golden Rules of Good Computing

Cybermanners follow the golden rule. Computer users should not send out to others what they would not like to receive. This can include rude or demeaning e-mail, annoying chain letters, deliberate hoaxes, and last, but certainly not least, destructive computer viruses.

What Is Netiquette?

Before traveling down the information superhighway, learning what is acceptable online behavior and what is not may help computer users avoid some embarrassing mistakes. Most Netizens appreciate polite behavior and will be more likely to respond to people who display it. Actions such as shouting, name-calling, and wasting people's time will not make anyone popular on or off the

Internet. Practicing cybermanners, on the other hand, may improve a teen's Internet interactions and make it less likely that communications are misunderstood or considered harassment.

Viruses—Nothing to Sneeze At

Downloading or sharing information. Visiting informative or entertaining Web sites. Sending e-mail or other forms of instant messages. These activities are what make using the Internet fun. Unfortunately, these activities can also make Internet users vulnerable to the dangers of computer viruses.

A computer virus is a computer program designed to infect files and create new copies of itself. In doing so, the virus can destroy everything in its path—including the files and systems that keep the computer running. Some computer viruses are benign, which means they do not cause any serious damage. Others are very destructive and can erase an entire hard drive.

For a long time, the odds of catching a computer virus were small, but the rate at which viruses are now being created is growing, and with that rate, the risk of being infected. According to CERT, a virus advisory organization, there were 53,000 computer viruses as of August 2000.[1]

Between 1996 and 1999, the average rate of virus infections among the world's computer users increased by 800 percent. While most of these viruses are just annoying, like the TP44 virus, which caused computers to play the song "Yankee Doodle Dandy" every day at 5 P.M., many of the new viruses can cause worldwide destruction.[2]

The FBI estimates that thirty new viruses are created each day, and it takes only a few hours for viruses to

Internetiquette

When sending e-mail, some online behavior has been known to make a teen look like an "e-diot."

- "SHOUTING!" Do not "shout." Messages that are typed in uppercase letters can be irritating to read. These messages are described by e-mailers as shouting. New e-mailers may not know this rule, so they may need to be told politely. An online shouter may need a gentle reminder. If he or she does not respond, an e-mailer can refuse to answer further messages until the other person tones it down.

- Before sending e-mail, read through it. Something that may sound funny if a person says it can sound rude or mean if written down. E-mail is often written so quickly that people do not stop to think about what they wrote.

- By the same token, messages from other people should be read through carefully. If people have left out punctuation or used a word with a double meaning, it might be easy to read the message as saying something different than what it was intended to say.

- Never post a message online without the permission of the person who wrote it. It is not nice and it could be illegal. A person should never pretend to be another person when sending messages.

- Do not curse. Do not be rude or vulgar. Swearing can get a person kicked off an Internet service. A whole family may also have its account canceled because of one member's online antics.

- Do not flame, that is, send messages designed to make people mad. Messages written in anger may seem like a good opportunity to vent feelings or an amusing way to create an argument at a Web site, but they tend to make the sender look immature.

- Do not ignite more flames by responding. Responding to a flame with an even harsher flame can cause a flame war. Flames are best ignored.

People who harass, threaten, or flame others can be banned from mailing lists or newsgroups, dropped by their Internet provider, sued, or even arrested.

crisscross the globe. The main way that viruses were spread a few years ago was through infected disks. Now viruses are also spread through e-mail attachments and can be hidden in video clips or behind the banner screens displayed on the top of Web sites. When viruses are spread through e-mail attachments, the virus may copy itself and then use the e-mail address book to send copies of itself to everyone on the e-mailing list.[3]

In a few hours a virus can do a lot of damage. A good example is the damage done by a virus known as the Love Bug (or Love Letter) virus, launched on May 4, 2000, by a computer student in Manila, the Philippines. The Love Bug virus persuaded people to open it with a message telling them that a love letter was enclosed. Later variations on this type of virus included a Joke virus, with the e-mail message "Very Funny" and a Happy Mother's Day virus, which thanked the receiver for spending hundreds of dollars on a Mother's Day diamond.

Within a day the Love Bug virus spread to more than twenty countries and caused $80 million in damage by destroying files. It affected five hundred thousand computer systems, including the United Nations' computer system.[4]

In the United States, people who create viruses can be prosecuted under a law known as the Computer Fraud and Abuse Act of 1996. The crimes covered by this law include using stolen passwords, transferring viruses, and obtaining unauthorized information through a computer. The recommended punishment for the crime is five years in prison and up to a $250,000 fine for damages. In some cases, this punishment might be applied to the damage done to each computer. With a virus like the Love Bug, the fines and jail time could really add up.[5]

Damage can be done by a virus before a person even

realizes that his or her computer has been infected. The Happy New Year's virus appeared when a person logged on. At that point, the words Happy New Year 1999 appeared along with a display of fireworks, which disguised the installation of the virus. By the time the fireworks were over, the virus had copied itself and been sent to everyone on the computer's e-mail list. The virus destroyed files. Software does exist to repair some of the damage done by viruses, but prevention remains the best cure.[6]

The National Computer Security Association estimates that if only 30 percent of computer owners regularly used up-to-date antiviral software, the virus problem would disappear.[7]

There are several ways to protect computers from viruses.

- Get antivirus protection. At least a dozen sites offer information about viruses and the software that can be used to fight them. Some virus protection is free.

- Stay up-to-date on the latest viruses. Antivirus software may need to be updated to deal with new viruses.

- Do not open e-mail attachments with ".vbs," ".com," and ".js." All contain a set-up for a virus that can be executed when the e-mail is opened.

- People who have Windows can disable a feature called Windows Scripting Host that runs vbs programs.

- Microsoft Outlook e-mail subscribers can disable the preview page in their e-mail programs. In this program you can see a preview of your message before opening it. When that preview appears, it can launch a virus.[8]

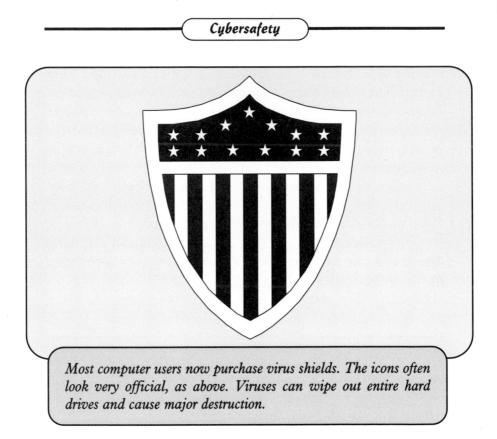

Most computer users now purchase virus shields. The icons often look very official, as above. Viruses can wipe out entire hard drives and cause major destruction.

Two other troublesome types of cybercreatures are worms and Trojan horses. Worms, like viruses, create new copies of themselves and spread from file to file, instead of from computer to computer. A Trojan horse is a destructive computer code concealed within a harmless code or data that is capable of taking control or causing damage. Unlike viruses or worms, Trojan horses do not make copies of themselves. Although they have different names because they spread differently, most people refer to worms, Trojan horses, and viruses under the general heading of viruses.

For every real virus, there are dozens of rumors about viruses that do not exist. Most people have received e-mail warnings of a potentially dangerous new virus.[9] One example is the rumored Good Times virus. Rumors about this virus have been circling the globe since 1994 and have been translated into almost every language, but the virus has never been proven to exist. Most sites that list dangers from real viruses will also post a list of virus hoaxes, but there are a few sites dedicated just to hoaxes.

Urban Myths Now Move at Warp Speed

Because e-mail makes communication so much faster, it also speeds up the rate at which the hoaxes known as urban myths or urban legends travel around the world.

Some urban e-mail legends are harmless pranks to see how fast and how far information can spread. Anger or jealousy can be a motive for starting damaging cyber-rumors. People with a grudge—such as people who worked for but were fired from a company—may create stories that create problems for that company. Examples of urban myths include the messages saying that Nike is giving out free shoes or the e-mail that Bill Gates will pay for a trip to Disneyland if a person forwards the message to enough of his or her friends.[10]

These steps may help combat the spread of e-mail hoaxes:

1. If the message seems suspicious, do not pass it on. Delete it.

2. Ask the sender how he or she can verify the message.

3. Use search engines to look for information about a suspected hoax.

4. Use verifiable sources. Go directly to the home page of the companies or government agencies.

5. Use common sense. If it sounds goofy, it probably is. One hoax claimed that people might soon be charged long distance rates for Internet use. If this story were really true, the news would almost certainly have been reported in newspapers or on television.[11]

4

Cybercrime

hile cybersurfers should protect their own safety online, they should also be careful not to hurt others. Some teens can become cybercriminals without even realizing they are breaking a law. Others may commit crimes like hacking, thinking that it is only a game and that they will never get caught. However, cybercrimes are taken seriously. New laws are being created to prosecute cybercriminals. New law enforcement divisions are being created to enforce these laws.

Illegally Copying Software

Uploading commercial software or other copyrighted material is illegal. Online libraries have lots of shareware (software which can used for a limited time for free), freeware (software which can be copied and used indefinitely

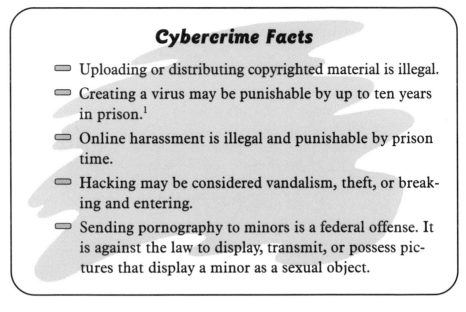

Cybercrime Facts

- Uploading or distributing copyrighted material is illegal.
- Creating a virus may be punishable by up to ten years in prison.[1]
- Online harassment is illegal and punishable by prison time.
- Hacking may be considered vandalism, theft, or breaking and entering.
- Sending pornography to minors is a federal offense. It is against the law to display, transmit, or possess pictures that display a minor as a sexual object.

for free), and material in the public domain (which is available for anyone to use). This material is not copyrighted (registered so that no one can use it without getting permission or paying a fee) and can be used by anyone. Materials that are copyrighted usually belong to the person who created them and may not be used without getting permission or paying a fee. In the case of recorded music, the copyright helps to ensure that the performers get paid.

Distributing copyrighted materials is also illegal, as is copying someone else's words and posting them on the Internet or using them on a Web site. Using copyrighted materials without permission is a form of theft.

Shawn Fanning was eighteen when he created the software for Napster, a music service that lets computer users connect to each other's computers for the purpose of downloading music. His music-copying company soon found itself the subject of several lawsuits, because it gave music fans instant access to hundreds of thousands of songs, many of them copyrighted. Fanning was sued by the Recording Industry Association of America (RIAA) and suits were filed by the heavy metal band Metallica and the rapper Dr. Dre. Fanning claimed that he was not responsible for what happened when people used his software, but the judge rejected this claim and the case went to trial.[2] In July 2000, U.S. District Court Judge Marilyn Patel ruled against Napster.[3] Napster appealed, but on February 12, 2001, the Ninth U.S. Circuit Court of Appeals ruled against Napster again.[4]

Cyberstalking

Harassing or stalking someone online is a crime just as much as harassing or stalking a person is in other situations. Using a computer to harass or stalk someone has been punishable by law since 1998. This harassment can take many forms. According to the CNETNews Web site, the first person arrested under this law was a fifty-year-old Los Angeles man. He was arrested in January 1999 for harassing a woman who turned down his romantic advances.

The harassment consisted of sending out e-mail messages in her name on America Online, inviting men to visit her for sex, and giving out her address. The victim did not even own a computer when the messages were posted. When she complained to the Los Angeles Police Department about the six men who visited her apartment, detectives were able to trace the messages back to the sender.[5]

Free Speech or Danger?

What can and cannot be said on the Internet remains open to discussion. The First Amendment of the United States Constitution protects the right of U.S. citizens to say what they want to on any subject, but how that right will be interpreted on the Internet is still being decided. In the United States, anyone can start a Web site and say what he or she likes. Even hate groups, including those that want to promote racism, have a right to start a Web site.

A pornographic Web site is legal as long as it does not feature pictures of children or is not marketed to minors. While pornography is not illegal, sending pornography to children is illegal. In an effort to protect children from having access to sexual material online, Congress recently passed the Communications Decency Act, which would limit the right to publish pornography online, but the Supreme Court decided this law was unconstitutional. That means the court decided that the law, however well intentioned, violated Americans' right to free speech as it is protected in the United States Constitution.

However, speech is not considered free if someone's life is in danger. Jake Baker, a University of Michigan student, was suspended from his university without a hearing for writing a fictional story that appeared in a Usenet group (a publicly accessed bulletin board).

The story described the murder of a female student whose name was the same as a student at the school. Baker was arrested even though he had never been in trouble before. Baker said he had no intention of carrying out the crime, but his fictitious story was considered a threat and a form of harassment because it could frighten his victim. A person has the right to express his thoughts and fantasies in fiction, however violent, but when Baker used the real name of the student, he may have crossed the line from fiction into real life.[6]

The U.S. Constitution protects the right of U.S. citizens to free speech, but how that right will be interpreted on the Web is still being decided. For example, the right to publish pornography online is being debated.

Hacking Is Not a Joke

A hacker was originally defined as a person who likes to spend time with computers or someone who creates computer software. It has come to mean someone who breaks or hacks into other people's computer systems. Hacking is a crime that can result in a prison sentence or, at the very least, the temporary taking away of any suspected criminal's computer equipment. It can be considered breaking and entering, theft, or fraud.

In January 2000, a nineteen-year-old Russian teen who calls himself Maxim sent an e-mail to *The New York Times* boasting that he had exploited a flaw in the software protecting financial information at a site called CD Universe, and had stolen files containing thousands of credit card numbers. He said he would destroy his credit card files in exchange for $100,000, but CD Universe said no. When the site refused to

Computer crime is a serious issue. Teens may think they are having fun when they steal someone's credit information or stalk someone online, but those are serious crimes punishable with fines and prison time.

cooperate, Maxim tried to post some of the numbers at an Internet site, but the FBI shut down the site. Credit card companies canceled and replaced the stolen credit card numbers. Maxim's real identity is still being investigated.[7]

Some hackers say that the people who commit these break-ins and cause this damage should be called crackers or criminal hackers. These hackers say that a true hacker is not interested in destruction and would not hurt anyone. They are only interested in new technology.[8]

Whatever they are called, hackers have done their share of virtual and physical damage. Some recent hacking break-ins include Web sites run by the U.S. Army, NASA, and the National Oceanic and Atmospheric Administration.[9]

Sometimes hackers break in and change the content of a company's or an organization's Web page, replacing the original contents with different images and words. Some break in and steal corporate secrets or national security information that can be sold to the highest bidder. In 1998, the FBI reported losses of nearly $124 million from computer security breaches.[10]

Cybercriminals can also break into home computers and steal personal and financial information. Increasingly, hackers are using home computers to get personal information, which could, for example, let them run up bills on the computer owners' credit cards. Cybercriminals can get access to information on a home computer by using special probing software that scans computers connected to the Internet. New high speed cable modems make it easier to hack into personal computers because these computers are always connected.

Some hackers have formed cybergangs with names such as the Cult of the Dead Cow, Global Hell, and Hacking for Girlies. Global Hell's founder, a Houston-based computer whiz with the online name of mosthated (his real name was withheld because he was a minor), was caught for taking an

FBI Web page out of action. When federal agents showed up at his home, mosthated had to face the unhappy task of explaining to his parents why the FBI was confiscating the family computer and all their financial records.[11]

Chad Davis, nineteen, the gang's co-founder, also had his home raided. Davis, also known as MindPhasr, said he was responsible for taking an FBI Web site out of action but never thought he would get caught. "I really wasn't expecting it to happen to me," said Davis, who had to give up his computer and three hundred CDs, onto which he may have copied software. He also had to pay a $165 fine.[12]

Fighting Cybercrime

As the incidence of cybercrime grows, so do the investigative skills and the number of agencies needed to track down online crimes. The National Infrastructure Protection Center (NIPC) was created within the FBI to protect the country's infrastructure systems—such as transportation, telecommunications, and water systems—from threats that include hacker attacks.

According to the NIPC, protecting the country from hackers is not just about the millions of dollars an e-commerce system can lose when these systems are shut down because of hacking. Hackers are also a threat to national security, as was shown in the case of Chameleon, the teen hacker who sold Defense Department software to terrorists for enough money to buy a Super Nintendo Game Boy.[13] The damage hackers do can affect anyone who has contact with the Internet.[14]

Can a person commit a crime such as hacking by accident?

It would be hard to hack by accident, says the NIPC. It is difficult. Even if a person gets lost while navigating the Net, that is not the same as damaging or destroying other people's property.[15]

5

How Teens Can Get Parents to Respect Their Privacy

*T*eens cherish their privacy. They want to be able to explore the Internet and discover new things on their own or with their friends. Parents want their children to be safe. But the differing needs of parents and teens do not have to create an unsolvable conflict. These needs can be a good basis for a contract in which both parents and teens clearly state what they feel comfortable with.

By establishing mutually plotted road rules for Net navigation, parents can be reassured that teens are safe online, and once reassured, may agree to let their teen have more online freedom and privacy.

First, teens should talk to their parents about how they spend time online and demonstrate the basics of Internet safety. Using the Internet together may help parents better understand teens' fascination with this medium and show parents that teens know what to look out for. Whether parents are new to the Net or are longtime techies, teens often know more about the Internet than their parents.

Teens and parents can create and sign an actual contract outlining what they consider to be responsible Internet use.

Even with the best intentions, accidents do happen. It can be easy to accidentally log on to a site parents may not approve of. If such a mistake happens, being completely honest can be the best way to keep the problem from getting worse. Otherwise, parents may wrongly assume the site was visited on purpose and may be angry at their innocent teen for not abiding by the agreed upon safety rules.

For example, what if Alyson accidentally logs on to a pornography site and, although she is upset, says nothing to her parents. One day her parents are looking for a site they visited on the computer and, on the computer's history of sites visited, they see a pornography site. As a result, Alyson's parents revoke her Internet privileges. She has to stay offline for a month and when she does get to use the Internet again, her mother always seems to be looking over her shoulder.

However, if Alyson discusses the incident with her parents when it happens, it could start a conversation that helps them see her as a responsible computer user. Her parents may ask if she did something to place herself in a dangerous position, such as logging on to a Web site that asks that all its members be over eighteen or if she gave another person the impression that she was interested in receiving this type of e-mail.

If so, they might discuss how she could have avoided the situation. If she received the pornography through no fault of her own, it is more likely they will only be upset with whoever sent the pornography. Knowing that such an incident happened can help parents and other concerned people try to keep a similar situation from happening in the future.

Ten Rules I Will Follow for Online Safety

1. I will not give out personal information about myself or my parents. This includes giving anyone an address or telephone number or my parents' work address or telephone number without my parents' permission.

2. I will never agree to talk to anyone I meet online on the telephone or to meet them without checking with my parents. If my parents agree to the meeting, it will be in a public place and one of my parents will come along.

3. I will never send anyone a picture of myself without checking with my parents.

4. I will not respond to messages that make me feel uncomfortable or are mean.

5. I will not get into a fight with anyone online; I will not swear or send insulting messages. If someone starts a fight with me, I will not respond.

6. I will not visit sites that I know my parents do not approve of.

7. I will tell my parents if I get any information that makes me feel uncomfortable. That includes pictures or e-mails using bad language or containing pornography.

8. I will not buy anything online without asking my parents. Nor will I give out credit card information. I will not fill out any forms without asking my parents' permission.

9. I will check for viruses whenever I borrow a disk or download from the Internet.

10. I will use a gender-neutral name in chat rooms and not give out any information that might help someone find me in real life.

_____ Teen

_____ Parent

Rules courtesy of *Teen Safety on the Information Superhighway,*
The National Center for Missing and Exploited Children.

Teens and their parents can work together to create a contract that outlines online safety rules.

Should Privacy Always Be Respected?

There are cases when a teen's privacy should not be respected. If a person is using the Internet to endanger himself or others, privacy becomes less important than that person's safety or the safety of others.

If it becomes clear that a friend or relative is using the Internet in a dangerous way, it is smart to tell a responsible adult. Examples of this type of dangerous activity might be when a teen uses the Internet to get information to build a bomb, when a teen plans a meeting with someone he or she met online, or when a friend is sending threatening e-mail messages. In these cases, it is important that the online activity stop before someone is hurt. Telling a caring adult about a situation that can threaten a friend is not "telling on" the friend. Getting help is what good friends do for each other. They try to help each other from hurting themselves or making other mistakes that could ruin their lives.

A person who is destructive or self-destructive usually needs professional help. If talking to parents is not an option, try talking to a minister or a school official, such as a guidance counselor or school psychologist. Some police officers may know a professional who specializes in such Internet-related situations. Or the situation can be reported to confidential hot lines or cyber-tip sites, which are set up for just this type of situation. Keeping quiet about a potentially dangerous situation does not help anyone.

Addicted to the Internet

Can a person be addicted to the Internet? A study of 17,251 Internet users investigated whether they were using time online to escape from their problems.[1]

For teens, compulsive use can mean that their Internet use lowers their grades, reduces the time spent participating in after-school activities, or causes teens to neglect family activities or chores. Too much time spent online may also indicate depression and an unwillingness to face everyday problems. Spending hours online is not addiction in and of itself, says Dr. David Greenfield, if a person is taking care of obligations and still getting enough sleep.[2]

Turning into a Nethead may not always have obvious warning signs, so listen to people who care. Complaints about too much time spent online are certainly worth thinking about. If spending time online always takes the place of reading a book, calling friends on the phone, or no longer doing homework, the Internet may be more than entertainment.

"Many people can deal with this issue without professional help," said Dr. Greenfield, "but first they have to recognize that it's a problem. Most often the person

According to Dr. David Greenfield, a psychologist who conducted an Internet use study, almost 6 percent of Internet users suffer from some sort of compulsion to be online. That meant they:

- had a hard time doing things other than spending time online
- found that the rest of their life was suffering as a result of Internet use
- thought about the Internet all the time, even when they were not online

Sometimes, the best thing to do is shut off the computer and take a walk with a friend.

recognizing the problem is not the person who is compulsive. It's usually a family member or friend. If you suspect that a person is compulsively using the Internet, it's important to confront the person and let them know your concerns."[3]

What should a person do when he or she finds that spending time online has become too much of a good thing? Shut off the computer for a while. Take a walk. Call a friend. At first it may seem odd not to be connected to the Net, but any change in habits takes some getting used to. If life offline seems too hard, get some help.

If a person suspects that any Internet behavior might endanger him or her or anyone else, it is important to discuss that behavior with someone trusted. Safe surfing starts with honest communication.

The Internet has become an important part of daily life and its uses will probably increase in importance during the next decade. An increasing number of people will use the Internet during their day at school or work and at home for entertainment. Not using the Internet because there are dangers could be compared to not crossing the street because traffic can be dangerous. When it comes to street traffic, it is a good idea to look both ways before crossing a street. The same is true for Internet use. Learning cybersafety rules and following them can help make surfing the Net a safer and more enjoyable experience.

Chapter Notes

Chapter 1. Cybersafety

1. Barbara Kantrowitz, "How Well Do You Know Your Kid?" *Newsweek*, May 10, 1999, p. 39.

2. Heather Moore, as told to Linda Marsa, "My Online Boyfriend Turned Out to Be a Pervert," *YM*, September 1999, pp. 106–108 (Moore is a pseudonym).

3. Associated Press, "Teens Accused of Internet Scam," *The Journal News*, N.J., January 13, 2000, p. 5A.

4. David Thelan, "How Teens Like Me Really Use the 'Net," *Computerworld* Web site, June 29, 1998, <http://www.computerworld.com> (May 14, 1999).

5. Kantrowitz, p. 39.

6. Daniel Okrent, "Raising Kids Online," *Time*, May 10, 1999, p. 42.

7. "Child Safety on the Information Highway," The National Center for Missing and Exploited Children, Arlington, Va., 1998, p. 4.

8. "Young Investor Web site Settles FTC Charges," Federal Trade Commission Web site, May 6, 1999, <http://www.ftc.gov> (May 19, 1999).

9. E-mail interview with Austin Lang, May 17, 1999.

10. E-mail interview with Emi Horikawa, May 15, 1999.

11. "Child Safety on the Information Highway," p. 5.

12. Sergio Bustos, "House Extends Stalking Law to Those Who Prey Online," *The Journal News*, November 11, 1999, p. 6A.

13. Matt Bai and T. Trent Gegax, "Searching For Answers," *Newsweek*, May 10, 1999, p. 33.

14. Bryan Burrough, "Invisible Enemies," *Vanity Fair*, June 2000, p. 214.

15. Parry Aftab, *A Parent's Guide to the Internet* (New York: SC Press, 1997), p. 111.

Chapter 2. How the Web Ensnares

1. Stacy Finz, "Cops Go Undercover Online to Nab Internet Pedophiles," *San Francisco Chronicle*, December 7, 1998, p. A21.

2. Parry Aftab, *A Parents' Guide to the Internet* (New York: SC Press, 1997), p. 85.

3. Marian Salzman and Robert Pondiscio, *Kids On-Line* (New York: Avon Camelot, 1995), p. 51.

4. Lawrence J. Magid, "Kids Need To Learn How To Sift Out Net Junk," July 12, 1999, <http://www.safekids.com> (February 1, 2000).

5. Sean Kelly and Karen E. Crummy, "Netting Sexual Predators: Law Enforcement Going Online To Catch Pedophiles Off-Guard," November 8, 1999, <http://www.denverpost.com> (February 1, 1999).

6. "Child Safety on the Information Highway," The National Center for Missing and Exploited Children, Arlington, Va., 1998, p. 12.

7. Interview with Alyson, September 4, 1999.

8. Vince Distefano and the staff of Classroom Connect, *Child Safety on the Internet* (Lancaster, Pa.: Prentice Hall, 1997), p. 218.

9. E-mail interview with Austin Lang, May 17, 1999.

10. Aftab, p. 15.

11. Robert B. Gelman, Stanton McCandish, and Esther Dyson, *Protecting Yourself Online: The Definitive Resource on Safety, Freedom and Privacy in Cyberspace* (New York: HarperEdge, HarperCollins, 1998), p. 46.

12. Daniel Tynan, "Privacy 2000: In Web We Trust?" *PC World*, June 2000, p. 106.

13. *Get Cyber Savvy*, The Direct Marketing Association, Washington, D.C., 1997, p. 15.

14. Tynan, p. 123.

15. Distefano, p. 141.

16. Ibid.

17. Daniel Okrent, "Raising Kids Online," CNN poll, *Time*, May 10, 1999, p. 42.

18. Distefano, p. 52.

19. Aftab, pp. 148–156.

20. "Cyberangels," n.d., <http://www.cyberangels.com> (November 26, 1999).

21. "CyberCops: Learning a New Beat," *Family PC Magazine*, n.d., <http://familypc.zdnet.com> (November 28, 1999).

Chapter 3. The Golden Rules of Good Computing

1. Computer Virus Advisory Organization, n.d., <http://www.cert.org> (August 14, 2000).

2. Lev Grossman, "The New HotZone," *Time*, July 11, 2000, <http://www.time.com> (August 14, 2000).

3. Saskia Wirth, "Internet Virus Threat: Who's Prepared?" 1997–2000, <http://www.CBS.MarketWatch.com> (August 14, 2000).

4. USA Today editors, "Evidence Lacking in Love Bug Case," 2000, <http://www.usatoday.com> (August 14, 2000).

5. Jim Geraghty, "The Global Fight Against Computer Viruses," July 31, 2000, <http://www.policy.com> (August 14, 2000).

6. Computer Virus Advisory Organization.

7. Good Times Virus Hoax Web site, <http://www.publicusit.net> (September 9, 1999).

8. Stephen Shankland, "How To Protect Your Computer From Viruses," May 19, 2000, <http://news.cnet.com> (August 14, 2000).

9. Good Times Web site.

10. Tina Kelley, "Internet's Chain of Foolery," *The New York Times*, July 1, 1999, p. G1.

11. Ibid.

Chapter 4. Cybercrime

1. Dean Takahashi and Don Clark, "Clues Conflict in the Hunt for Originals of Fast-Moving E-Mail Computer Virus," *Wall Street Journal* Interactive Edition, n.d., <http://interactive.wsj.c> (September 30, 1999).

2. John Borland, "Napster to Face Trial on Music Piracy Claims," May 18, 2000, <http://www.CNETNews.com> (August 14, 2000).

3. Karl Taro Greenfield, "Meet the Napster," *Time*, October 2, 2000, p. 66.

4. Mark Ward, "Why MP3 Piracy Is Much Bigger Than Napster," BBC News, February 13, 2001, <http://news.bbc.co.uk/hi/english/sci/tech/newsid_1168000/1168087.stm> (February 13, 2001).

5. Dan Goodin, "Cyberstalking Laws Snag Alleged Violator," January 25, 1999, <http://news.cnet.com/news/0-1005-200-33787.html> (August 15, 2000).

6. Robert B. Gelman, Stanton McCandish, and Esther Dyson, *Protecting Yourself Online: The Definitive Resource on Safety, Freedom and Privacy in Cyberspace* (New York: HarperEdge, HarperCollins, 1998), pp. 29–30.

7. Ibid., p. 28.

8. Brendan Koerner, "Who Are Hackers Anyway?" *U.S. News and World Report*, June 14, 1999, p. 53.

9. Ann Harrison and Kathlenn E. Ohlson, "Crackers Used Known Weakness On Fed Sites," *Computerworld*, July 5, 1999, vol. 33, p. 1.

10. Brendan Koerner, Doug Pasternak, and David Kaplan, "Can Hackers Be Stopped?" *U.S. News and World Report*, June 14, 1999, p. 46.

11. Ibid.

12. Chris Taylor, "Geeks Vs G-Men," *Time*, June 14, 1999, p. 64.

13. Bryan Burrough, "Invisible Enemies," *Vanity Fair*, June 2000, p. 210.

14. Telephone interview with supervisory special agent, National Infrastructure Protection Center, December 17, 1999 (name withheld).

15. Ibid.

Chapter 5. How Teens Can Get Parents to Respect Their Privacy

1. "Child Safety on the Information Highway," The National Center for Missing and Exploited Children, Arlington, Va., 1998.

2. Interview with Dr. David Greenfield, February 18, 2000.

3. Ibid.

Glossary

antivirus program—Software designed to guard against, detect, and remove viruses.

AOL—America Online, the biggest Internet provider.

AIM—AOL Instant Messenger, a form of real-time electronic conversation.

browser—A program such as Netscape Navigator or Microsoft's Internet Explorer that lets computer users surf the Web.

chat room—An online room in which people can talk to each other by typing in their words.

cracker—A criminal hacker (see **hacker**).

cyberspace—The world of information available through computer networks.

database—A collection of computer files that contain information.

e-mail—Electronic mail; messages sent via computers.

file—Information stored on a computer as a unit.

firewall—Filtering software designed to keep hackers and viruses out, used by online businesses for security.

flame—An abusive or personally insulting electronic message.

hacker—An expert in computer technology and system codes. Also, a person who uses computer expertise illegally; for example, to gain access to computer systems without permission (see **cracker**).

icon—A picture on the computer screen that gets clicked on by the mouse and opens a program.

ISP—Stands for Internet service provider or the connection with which a person reaches the Internet.

netiquette—Internet etiquette.

netizen—A person who communicates online.

network—A system that lets linked computers exchange information.

newsgroups—Online discussion groups on a particular subject.

online—The term used for communication with another computer.

real time—Something that happens online in the same time it would happen in real life; for example, a conversation.

search engine—A special Web site used to locate information based on specific keywords.

spamming—Using a mailing list to send mail, usually advertisements, to a large number of people.

Trojan horse—Malicious computer code concealed within harmless code or data.

viruses—Programs that travel from computer to computer via floppy disks, networks, or telecommunications systems. Viruses alter and can damage computer data.

Web site—A group of Web pages with a specific sponsor, such as a local library.

World Wide Web—The part of the Internet that can be viewed using a browser.

worm—Destructive cybercreature similar to a virus that does not need a carrier program to spread.

Further Reading

Dixon, Pam. *Take Charge Computing for Teens and Parents*. Foster City, Calif.: IDG Books Worldwide, 1996.

Gralla, Preston. *The Complete Idiot's Guide to Protecting Yourself Online*. New York: Que Publishing, Macmillan, 1999.

Levine, John R., Carol Baroudi, and Margaret Levine. *The Internet for Dummies*. Foster City, Calif.: IDG Books Worldwide, 2000.

Mandel, Mimi. *The Teen's Guide to the World Wide Web*. Fort Atkinson, Wisc.: Highsmith Press, 1999.

McConnell, Sharon. *The Everything Internet Book*. Holbrook, Mass.: Adams Media Corporation, 1998.

Merkle, Robert. *The Ultimate Internet Terrorist: How Hackers, Geeks and Phreaks Can Ruin Your Trip on the Information Superhighway and What You Can Do To Protect Yourself*. Boulder, Colo.: Paladin Press, 1998.

Schwartau, Winn. *Cybershock: Surviving Hackers, Phreakers, Identity Thieves, Internet Terrorists and Weapons of Mass Disruption*. New York: Thunder's Mouth Press, 2000.

Internet Addresses

Safety Tips

Cyberangels

This organization patrols the Internet and works with the NMEC and other law enforcement organizations.

> <www.cyberangels.org>

Enough is Enough

An Internet safety organization that protects kids from illegal pornography sites and predators.

> <www.enough.org>

Microsoft

A list of 30 Ways To Stay Safe Online.

> <http://encarta.msn.com/schoolhouse/safety.asp>

Safesurfin

An Internet driver's education course and other useful information sponsored by America Online and the American Library Association.

> <www.safesurfin.com>

SafeTeens.com

By *Los Angeles Times* columnist and Internet safety expert, Lawrence J. Magid, sponsored by AOL.

> <www.safeteens.com>

To Report a Crime

Cybertipline.com

The National Center for Missing and Exploited Children works on behalf of missing and exploited children.

> <www.missingkids.com/cybertip>

Spam Information

Fight Spam on the Internet
Works to boycott spam.

> <www.spam.abuse.net>

SpamCop
Lets computer users track spam back to its source and report it to the authorities.

> <spamcop.net>

Hoaxes

About.Com/Urban Legends and Folklore
Tracks Web hoaxes.

> <urbanlegends.about.com>

Don't Spread That Hoax!
Information to help users spot a hoax.

> <www.nonprofit.net/hoax>

HoaxKill
Information to help users spot a hoax.

> <www.hoaxkill.com>

Fraud Protection

The Better Business Bureau
A source for information on businesses and a place to file complaints.

> <www.bbb.org>

The Center for Democracy and Technology Snooper 2.0
Lets a user see what kinds of information a computer can automatically record from a simple site visit.

> <http://snoop.cdt.org>

The Direct Marketing Association
Offers information on Internet shopping and marketing.

> <www.the-dma.org>

The National Fraud Information Center
Tips to protect users against online fraud.

<www.fraud.org>

Hacking Dangers

National Infrastructure Protection Center
Created by President Clinton to fight Internet terrorism internationally.

<www.nipc.gov>

Netiquette
Offers tips on e-mail etiquette.

<www.bpl.org/www/KIDS/Netiquette.html>

Virus Protection Information

CERT
Computer Virus Advisory Organization

A summary of the most frequent and serious commercial security incidents.

<www.cert.org>

Trend Micro
Lists current viruses and has a virus encyclopedia.

Index

A
antivirus software, 33

C
chat rooms, 5–6, 12, 13,
16–17, 19
cookies, 20–21, 22
credit card transactions,
21–23, 42–43, 47
CyberAngels, 27–28
cybercrime, 13–14, 27–28, 32,
37–44
cybermanners, 29–30

D
domain names, 24–25

E
e-mail, 8, 10, 17, 18, 19, 20,
26, 28, 30, 31, 32, 33, 35,
39, 47, 49

F
firewalls, 23
flaming, 12, 31
freeware, 37

G
giving out personal
information, 5–8, 17–18,
47

H
hacking, 7–8, 13–14, 22, 23,
37, 38, 42–44
harassment, 9, 10, 13, 19, 28,
30, 47
hatred and racism online,
25–26, 40
hoaxes, 35–36

I
Internet addiction, 49–50, 52

L
Love Bug virus, 32

M
meeting people online, 5–7,
9–10, 16–18
misinformation online, 23–24

N
Napster, 38–39
netiquette, 29–30
newsgroups, 12, 31

P
password use, 19
pedophiles, 9–10, 15–18

S
scams, 7–8, 19–20
screening systems, 26–27
screen names, 11–12

secure sites, 21–23

shareware, 37

software copying, 37–39

spamming, 11–12, 19–20

stalking, 13, 39

T

Trojan horses, 34

V

violence promoted online, 25–26

viruses, 9, 10, 14, 30, 32–35, 38

W

Web browsing programs, 20-21

worms, 34